Art Treasures
of the United Nations

ART TREASURES OF THE UNITED NATIONS

By Jacob Baal-Teshuva

With a Foreword By Andrew W. Cordier

New York • THOMAS YOSELOFF • London

To my sisters
Ruth and Mina

Foreword

THIS BOOK ON THE ART OBJECTS THAT EMBELLISH THE UNITED NATIONS HEADQUARTERS buildings should be of interest to many readers. When the design of the buildings was under question by a distinguished group of world architects, headed by Mr. Wallace Harrison, much thought was given to the desirability of adding further accents of beauty through works of art that might be contributed by members of the United Nations or by private sources.

The new buildings were occupied in 1950 and some of the paintings and murals that were a part of the original planning were completed at the time of occupancy. These included the Léger paintings in the General Assembly hall and the mural by Per Krohg in the Security Council chamber. The beautiful Belgian tapestry was hung in the General Assembly building soon thereafter.

In the years that followed, the United Nations received a number of art objects that added further to the richness of the buildings. Perhaps the two most widely appreciated of these gifts bore a stamp of great age, though despite their age they do not seem to contradict the modernity of the construction. They are the beautiful third-century mosaic, the gift of the government of Tunisia, and the lovely Peruvian tapestry presented by that government — a tapestry some 2900 years old.

All other gifts belong to the modern school of painting and sculpture. There are the imaginative frescoes of Bo Beskow — the first, a frontispiece in the Meditation Room and the second, a gay mural in the penthouse of the Dag Hammarskjöld Library. The artistry of Fritz Glarner is reflected in his large mural at the entrance to the Dag Hammarskjöld Library. A French tapestry, taken from a painting by Picasso, graces the Security Council lounge; a mural by José Vela Zanetti of the Dominican Republic is regularly viewed by thousands of visitors on the third floor lobby of the conference building. Among the most radical of the murals are those by Portinari of Brazil which cover the large wings of the delegates entrance.

Dag Hammarskjöld's taste for modern art was reflected in the sculptural pieces by Martinelli, on the east side of the Assembly hall, by Robert Cronbach in the anteroom of the Meditation Room, and by José de Rivera in the Secretary-General's office.

7

Recently a modern mosaic, copied from an older design — a gift of the King of Morocco — was located in the neck between the General Assembly and the conference buildings.

Attention has had to be given during the years to the acceptance of gifts which would represent appropriate and valued additions to the decor of the United Nations headquarters. It is generally felt that, despite the difficulty, adjustment of varied artistic creations to a beautiful modern architectural design has been achieved with a considerable degree of success.

Andrew W. Cordier, Dean, School of International
Affairs, Columbia University, and former Under-
Secretary for General Assembly Affairs

Acknowledgments

MANY OF THE PHOTOGRAPHS REPRODUCED IN THIS BOOK ARE FROM THE UNITED NATIONS photographic section and photo library, and the United Nations Publishing Service. My thanks to Miss Selma Van der Molen, Mr. Drago Vujica, Director of the Yugoslav Information Center, Mr. C. M. Wei of the Mission of China to the United Nations, Mr. Zaman of the Pakistan Mission to the United Nations, and the staffs of the Metropolitan Museum of Art, and the UNICEF Greeting Card Fund for their aid. I am especially indebted to Mr. Andrew W. Cordier, Dean of the School of International Affairs at Columbia University and former Under-Secretary for General Assembly Affairs for his Foreword. To all of them my deep appreciation and thanks.

J. B.-T.

New York, September 1963

Contents

Art Treasures
of the United Nations

Art gives more to life than it takes from it. True art does not depend on the reality about which it tells, its message lies in the new reality which it creates, by the way in which it reflects experience.

—Dag Hammarskjöld

Art Treasures of the United Nations

THE UNITED NATIONS HEADQUARTERS, THE COMPLEX OF LANDSCAPED GROUNDS AND modern buildings overlooking Manhattan's East River, has been described as "the nearest thing to a world capital yet achieved by man." It has become a major tourist attraction, drawing millions of people from every corner of the world, and it has become a museum of the arts, displaying in its architecture, murals, paintings, mosaics, tapestries and sculptures the ancient heritage and modern talents of many lands.

The buildings are the physical embodiment of the United Nations, an organization of 113 member states dedicated to the goals of peace, freedom, and equal opportunity for all. Created by the combined architectural talent of a brilliant international team, the buildings rise from their setting of landscaped gardens to dominate the East River skyline.

The history of this unique complex is well known to millions of tourists. When the first session of the United Nations General Assembly, meeting in London in 1946, approved the United States as the permanent home of the organization, Philadelphia, Boston, and San Francisco were the cities most favored as possible locations. The dramatic offer by John D. Rockefeller, Jr., of a gift of $8,500,000 made possible the purchase of the site and brought the United Nations to New York. A long-range program of landscaping and improvement of the area was undertaken by the City of New York, to give the organization a suitable setting for its great task.

The property thus acquired by the United Nations was a dreary and unimpressive area of the waterfront. Its ancient streets were lined with factories, breweries, and dilapidated tenements, affording no hint of its historic past. Here, in 1639, the Director-General of the colony of New Netherland authorized the establishment by two English tobacco growers of the plantation that became known as the Turtle Bay Farm, from an indentation of the East River shoreline in the area.

The area figured prominently in the American Revolution, and it was on this site that Nathan Hale gave his life as a patriot-spy. During the nineteenth century

The permanent headquarters of the United Nations in New York. The Secretariat is at the right of the picture, the Dag Hammarskjöld Library is in the foreground, and the General Assembly building is in the background.

the Turtle Bay area became a fashionable residential area, but in the latter part of the century, as the city made its way "uptown," the character of the site changed, giving way to commercial buildings and squalid tenements.

The site acquired, the United Nations organization moved quickly to plan and erect its headquarters structures. Early in 1947, Wallace K. Harrison, an American architect, was appointed to direct the planning. Outstanding architects from ten countries were appointed to form a consultant board: Charles E. Le Corbusier of France, N. D. Bassov of Russia, Gaston Brunfaut of Belgium, Ernest Cormier of Canada, Liang Ssu Cheng of China, Sven Markelius of Sweden, Oscar Niemeyer of

16

Brazil, Howard Robertson of England, G. A. Soilleux of Australia, and Julio Vilamajo of Uruguay.

Faced with the problem of combining beauty with utility, the architects devoted three-quarters of the eighteen acres comprising the site to gardens, trees, and lawns, which left no place to go but up. Completed in 1952, the tall and narrow thirty-nine-story secretariat contrasts structurally with the long, low building of marble and limestone that houses the General Assembly. Two other structural units complete the complex—the conference building that houses the chambers of the Security Council, the Economic and Social Council and the Trusteeship Council, and the new six-story library.

Aluminum, glass, and marble were used exclusively on the broad east-west façades of the secretariat, which rises 505 feet above the street level. Wide expanses of green tinted glass are unbroken by conventional setbacks. In sharp contrast, the narrow north-south façades are windowless and are faced with 2,000 tons of Vermont marble.

The approach to the headquarters complex forms a 400-foot arc, over which fly the flags of the member nations in a colorful border when the General Assembly is in session. Before the secretariat is a circular fountain, erected with a fund of $50,-000.00 donated by the children of the United States. At the base of the fountain is a pool, the floor of which displays a wavy pattern of alternating white crushed marble and black pebbles, gathered by women and children on the beaches of the island of Rhodes.

The assembly building, both in its exterior and interior, is the product of many countries. Limestone for its façade came from England, marble from Italy, stone from Israel. Its interior furnishings came from France, Greece, and Czechoslovakia, its carpets from the looms of Scotland, its woodwork from the Philippines, Cuba, Guatemala, Norway, Belgium, and Canada.

The United Nations was planned to bring together the nations of the world politically, economically, socially, and culturally. Almost from the beginning, it has been concerned with the arts of its member nations and along with its development as an unprecedented political forum, it has also become a repository of world art. Today murals, paintings, sculpture, tapestries, rugs, woodwork, and mosaics, ancient and modern, decorate the chambers of discussion, debate, and contemplation. Works by Picasso, Léger, Dufy, Portinari, Matisse and many others lend beauty, color, and inspiration to the atmosphere of international diplomacy.

All of the art objects owned by the United Nations were donated by the member states or by private organizations or individuals, who took this means of expressing appreciation of the efforts of the international assembly. A special advisory board appointed by the secretary-general passed upon each proferred gift, to determine its suitability for acceptance by the United Nations.

While the works donated cover a wide range of subject and design, many express themes representing the objectives of the organization — peace, international justice, and human rights.

Any survey of the art treasures of the United Nations must start with the nine great murals that adorn the walls of the headquarters buildings, representing work by artists from France, Brazil, Norway, Sweden, the Dominican Republic, and the United States. Of these the best known are the twin murals designed by Fernand Léger for the plenary hall of the General Assembly.

The plenary hall of the General Assembly building with Léger's mural number one on the right hand side, and mural two on the left hand side.

This great auditorium measures 380 by 160 feet, but despite its enormous size, the sloping walls and domed ceiling create an effect of intimacy. The room was designed to focus attention on the speaker occupying the rostrum, and the impressive effect of the room is enhanced by the two murals, each about thirty feet square, which flank the rostrum on the east and west walls. The murals are the gift of an anonymous donor, presented through the American Association for the United Nations. These murals, among the last of Léger's work, were designed in small sketches, eight inches square, and were executed in 1952 by the American artist, Bruce Gregory, of Philadelphia, who had studied with Léger in Paris for two years. Léger had the deep satisfaction of realizing their completion just three years before his death at the age of seventy-four.

The mural on the west wall is painted in "cadmium yellow medium, toned down, 'United Nations blue,' and white, on a dark gray background," according to the official release, while the one on the east wall is executed in "cadmium orange, white and gray, on a dark gray background."

The general assembly building houses also the two largest murals. These are by the eminent Brazilian, Candido Portinari, and are installed in the south lobby on the ground floor of the building. Measuring 34 by 46 feet each, the murals were

18

Fernand Léger's mural number one.

Fernand Léger's mural number two.

offered as a gift from Brazil in 1952, and were accepted by the advisory board from sketches supplied by the artist. The murals were completed in 1955 and 1956, having been executed in oils on cedar plywood. The mural depicting "War" is executed in dark, morbid colors, while "Peace" on the opposite wall is painted in warm and colorful pigments. The artist, in describing his murals, said, "War today is no longer a battlefield; it is human suffering, torn fields, ruined cities, women and children sacrificed, the world shaken by cataclysm; its desolation is swept by a wind of insanity, of madness . . ." In executing the mural depicting peace, Portinari

Portions of Portinari's War and Peace murals are seen prior to their being mounted.

explained that he was inspired by the ideal atmosphere of serenity of the spirits described in *Eumenides* by Aeschylus, and he sought, "following a parallel suggestion, to make use of simple and pure forms, bathed in a light capable of suggesting an atmosphere of brotherhood and understanding among men."

The chamber of the Security Council is one of the most beautiful rooms in the headquarters buildings. The room was designed by Arnstein Arenberg of Norway, and the Norwegian government contributed the decor and furnishings. The dominant feature of the room is a large mural, 16 by 26 feet, designed and exe-

21

The late Dag Hammarskjöld, Ambassador Cyro de Freitas-Valle, Representative of Brazil to the United Nations, and M. Jayme de Barros, Deputy Representative of Brazil, examine the Portinari murals.

cuted by the Norwegian artist Per Krohg. Here too the artist depicted the symbols of war and peace—the evils of the world that we are forsaking, painted in sinister shades of verdigris, rust, and still-blue, and the world we hope to attain, painted in light, bright colors and ascending lines. "I have tried," Krohg said, "not to use the ordinary, hackneyed symbols. Freedom is a man taking away a horse's bit and letting him run free in the green meadows. Brotherhood is shown by the union of nations and races in the central panels. The whole is lighted by the sun's rays. A small horizontal panel at the top, which I call the new renaissance, contains all the arts happily united, the men who interpret events and develop them, those who write history. In the center is an oval panel which I call peace. Two persons kneel face

22

A Per Krohg mural on display in the Security Council chamber.

to face, surrounded by children. War is over, a great calm enfolds them, they are at peace."

Man's struggle for peace and freedom from superstition is the theme of the great mural in the third-floor lobby of the conference building. Designed and executed by José Vela Zanetti, of the Dominican Republic, it is more than 60 feet long and 10 feet high. It was painted directly on the canvas-covered, curved wall. The artist himself offered the design, which was accepted in June, 1952, and the execution of the mural was made possible by a fellowship of the John Simon Guggenheim Memorial Foundation. Zanetti, not yet forty years old at the time, did all of the work himself, painting seven days a week, often far into the night, in a period of five months.

Zanetti's work is direct, forceful, clear. "Allegories tend to limit the sphere of action in murals," he said. "It is better to show things the meaning of which will be easily grasped by everyone." The mural begins at the left with the destruction of a family and ends at the right with its resurrection and a bright-eyed child look-

23

José Vela Zanetti at work on his mural for the Conference building.

ing toward a generation of peace. In the left panel concentration camps, bombings, all the agony of modern war are depicted. In the center a giant four-armed figure implants the emblem of the United Nations, and the symbols of justice, reconstruction, and human rights dominate the right side.

The Meditation Room, for the use of delegates and visitors, to the west of the public lobby of the General Assembly building, is unique in concept. Dedicated to peace, it is a room of quiet, "where only thoughts should speak." In the center of the room is a great slab of raw iron ore, chosen as a symbol of timelessness and strength. The rock is four feet high and weighs six tons, thus being probably the largest single slab of this crystalline ore ever to be extracted. It is a gift of the Swedish government.

24

Zanetti worked for five months on his mural, which depicts "man's struggle for peace and his fight against superstition."

A fresco panel occupies the front wall off the V-shaped room. The fresco, painted on wet plaster by the Swedish artist Bo Beskow, covers a projecting panel nine feet high and six and one-half feet wide. It is an abstract composition in blue, white, gray, and yellow geometric forms, with light pure colors intersecting to form deeper shades.

The choice of an abstract mural here was deliberate. Dag Hammarskjöld explained the choice: "We all have within us a center of stillness surrounded by silence. This house, dedicated to work and debate in the service of peace, should have one room dedicated to silence in the outward sense and stillness in the inner sense. It has been the aim to create in this small room a place where the doors may be open to the infinite lands of thought and prayer. People of many faiths will meet

25

A fresco by Swedish artist, Bo Beskow, is placed slightly in advance of the front wall of the Meditation Room.

here, and for that reason none of the symbols to which we are accustomed in our meditation could be used."

In designing the fresco, the artist sought "to open up the room so that the eye can travel in the distance when it strikes the wall." To give the effect of upward movement he designed widening circles and a spiralling diagonal line which might be compared to a vibrating musical chord. As a resting point for the viewer's eye, he provided one spot of black amid the lighter colors, a half-circle at which all the lines of the fresco and the room converge. The fresco is the gift of an anonymous donor.

Bo Beskow putting the finishing touches on his mural for the Hammarskjöld Library.

Beskow's work is also represented in the mural which is the sole wall decoration in the penthouse of the new Dag Hammarskjöld Library. The library, the gift of the Ford Foundation, is a building of white marble, glass, and aluminum, six stories and penthouse, to house some 400,000 volumes. The library is connected with the secretariat on two levels, and in addition to the stacks and the reading rooms, it contains a small auditorium designed like a Greek amphitheatre. The mural by Beskow, an abstract composition, measuring 26 by 14 feet, is executed in oils on canvas and is mounted on a concave wall at the west end of the penthouse lounge.

27

It is a colorful and joyous composition, which the artist has called simply "Composition for Concave Wall."

The concept, the artist explained, is quite different from that of the fresco in the Meditation Room. The penthouse lounge is "a room full of light, where you are very conscious of Manhattan outside." The lounge was planned to be used for festive occasions, and it called for a strong and colorful concept. The execution is in clear, vivid colors, the background predominantly a vibrant blue, and the diverse forms in white, yellow, black and varying shades of strong purple, red, and green.

"Composition for a Concave Wall" in place in the Penthouse Lounge of the Library.

In the eye of the beholder viewing the mural the forms may be interchanged and regrouped at will within the framework of the whole composition. (This work may be seen reproduced in color in the plate section of this volume.)

The library also houses a mural by the American artist Fritz Glarner. "Relational Painting Number 90" is an abstract design in geometric forms, strongly reminiscent of Mondrian. Slightly more than 11 feet in length and 22 feet high, it occupies a wall panel facing an ornamental terrazzo marble staircase leading from the main lobby of the building to the auditorium below. The mural is a colorful decoration, in blue, yellow, white, black, red, and gray.

Fritz Glarner working on his mural for the United Nations Library.

The Glarner mural in place in the main lobby of the Hammarskjöld Library.

Glarner was a favorite artist of Dag Hammarskjöld, and it is appropriate that his mural should have been chosen as one of the works of art in the library. The artist, in describing his work, has said: "My concern in painting has been to bring about a purer and closer inter-relation between form and space. The slant or oblique which I have introduced in my paintings determines the space and liberates the form. This may be seen clearly in the circle, the strongest form symbol of oneness. A multiplicity of similar quadrilaterals, one side of each, a segment of the circumference, establishes the structure and becomes one with the space. Differentiation is established by the opposition of color and space area, and the receding and advancing properties of various colors which give a new kind of depth to the space. Differentiation of textures disturbs the unity of a painting of pure relationship. The same texture should be maintained throughout the work. It is my conviction that this relational painting is part of a step-by-step development toward the essential integration of all plastic art."

President Habib Bourguiba of Tunisia presented an ancient mosaic master-piece to the late Dag Hammarskjöld during a visit to the United States in 1961.

In addition to the nine conventional murals in the United Nations collection, two large mosaics have been mounted for mural display. The first of these, an ancient Tunisian work of the third century, was discovered at Haidra, Tunisia, a quarter of a century ago. It is a gift of the Tunisian government, and was presented by President Habib Bourguiba, in a personal visit in May, 1961. Measuring eleven feet square, it has been mounted on a wall inside the entrance to the delegates' north lounge. Its design is typical of the Roman symbolism of the period — a personification of nature. In the center a nude boy stands within a circle representing the zodiac, in his right hand a sheaf of wheat. In each corner a winged cupid stands within a circular frame, each representing a season of the year. Thus the spring cupid stands before a luxuriant rosebush, with a peacock and a peahen at his sides. Summer stands in a field of wheat, with pheasants beside him. Autumn stands in a vineyard, with herons, and winter, snugly wrapped in a woollen cloak, carries a brace of ducks and a birdlime snare amid olive branches, with two geese at his

31

sides. The whole design is given a feeling of unity by the plants which spread inward from the corners to the center, characteristic of the original, spontaneous, and almost romantic style of the African genius of the period. Because of the happy and optimistic feeling of the design, the work is believed to antedate the devastation wrought by Capellien's troops in 238 A.D.

The second mosaic panel, a gift of the government of Morocco, was executed for this purpose by an old artist in Fez, Morocco. Presented by King Hassan II, in the course of an official visit to the United Nations in April, 1963, it has been

King Hassan II, of Morocco (front of microphone) presents a Mosaic panel to Secretary General U Thant. The panel is done in the Andalusian style of the twelfth century.

erected in the area connecting the General Assembly building with the conference building. The colorful mosaic has been executed in the traditional Andalusian style of the twelfth century, with an intricate woodwork frame surrounding the mosaic inset. It bears three inscriptions. The first, carved at the top, in the wooden frame, is the Surat El-Hujurat from the Koran: "O, mankind, we created you from a male and a female and made you into nations and tribes, that ye may know each other. The most honored of you in the sight of Allah is the most righteous of you." The preamble of the United Nations charter appears in Arabic script in the upper por-

A section of the granite wall-facing in the United Nations plaza area.

Arkady A. Sobolev, Representative of the U.S.S.R. to the United Nations, speaks at the unveiling of the statue, "Let Us Beat Swords Into Ploughshares."

tion of the mosaic panel, against a green background, and within this area is a red circle bearing the legend in bold Arabic script: "Charter of the United Nations." This mosaic is notable also in that it was the first work of art presented to the United Nations in the tenure of the third secretary-general, U Thant.

Nine sculptures, representing work by artists from Russia, Yugoslavia, Denmark, Indonesia, Greece, and the United States, are now on view in the United Nations headquarters. Most of these, like the murals, reiterate the themes of peace and cooperation among nations.

The equestrian statue symbolizing peace, presented by the government of Yugoslavia, stands in the north garden of the United Nations.

In the north rose garden stands the symbolic sculpture, "We Shall Beat Our Swords into Ploughshares," a gift of the Soviet Union. This powerful work by the Russian sculptor Evgeniy Viktorovich Vuchetich received the highest award, the Grand Prix, at the Brussels International Exposition in 1958, and was presented to the United Nations the following year. Described as a work of "socialist realism," it is in fact classical in its heroic power. Its symbolism is patent and clear, following the Soviet trend in art, and its message of hope for the triumph of peace over war is brought home daily to the thousands of visitors to the garden.

Also in the north garden is the equestrian sculpture "Mir" (peace) by Antun

Augustincic of Yugoslavia. This work, a gift of the Yugoslav government, is cast in bronze, 16 feet in height, and it is mounted on a 26-foot pedestal of rose marble quarried in Yugoslavia. The figure is an equestrienne, her left arm outstretched, her left hand holding an olive branch, the traditional symbol of peace. In her right hand rests a globe, the symbol of the world. The artist worked for two years in the execution of the sculpture, and he was present when the work was unveiled at the United Nations.

From the government of Denmark came the painted wooden sculpture which stands in the chamber of the Trusteeship Council. The furnishings of this room were a gift from the Danish government, which sponsored a competition for a suitable sculpture. The winner was one of Denmark's leading artists, Henrik Starcke, who carved this beautiful and colorful symbolic figure. The sculpture stands nine and a half feet high, the figure of a young woman dressed in a patterned robe, with arms upraised toward a large blue bird with wings spread. In a note explaining the conception of the work, the artist wrote: "As the natural growth of the trunk of the tree, used in the sculpture, gives promise of a still greater life, so do I hope to inspire in those present the realization of the great human dream. The bird above the figure, with its wings spread, suggests unlimited flight upward to greater heights. The arms of the figure itself are spread out in the same spirit as the wings of the bird, and I hope this might convey the appeal for compassion for the weak, the unfortunate, the oppressed."

Two Balinese sculptures in wood are the gift of the government of Indonesia. The two figures, each measuring about three feet in height, represent "Peace" and "Prosperity," and stand in the southwest foyer of the General Assembly Hall.

The figure of "Peace" is by an anonymous Balinese artist and is executed in satinwood. It depicts a *pedanda*, a Balinese priest, in traditional costume, with hands folded in ritual prayer. "Prosperity" is the work of I Made Runda, and depicts a woman wearing the large earstuds of the prosperous Balinese, carrying on her head a basket of rice paddy, surmounted by an image of Devi Sri, the rice goddess, who is also the goddess of prosperity. In her right hand the woman carries a paddy strainer, while her left hand holds her sarong in graceful folds. This figure is carved out of a single piece of "Bentawas" wood.

The Greek government offered as a gift the figure of Zeus, which stands in the public lobby of the General Assembly building. This work is a replica of a classic sculpture of about 460 B.C., which was discovered in recent years and which is now in a museum in Athens. The copy is seven feet high and is mounted on a marble pedestal. It depicts Zeus, king of the gods of Greek mythology, as a bearded young man with the classic body of an athlete, his right hand outstretched in the characteristic pose of the javelin-thrower. This work was one of the first to be presented to the United Nations, and was accepted on February 20, 1953, by the first secretary-general, Trygve Lie.

Dag Hammarskjöld (foreground), and Dr. Eelco N. van Kleffens, President of the General Assembly during its 1954-55 term, admiring the sculpture of "Prosperity."

"Zeus," in the main lobby of the General Assembly building.

Three contemporary American sculptures complete the United Nations Collection. These were presented by the National Council for United States Art, and are the work of three leading American sculptors, Ezio Martinelli, Robert Cronbach and José de Rivera. The three designs were submitted in a competition for an appropriate sculpture for the anteroom of the Meditation Room. All three of the designs submitted were of such high merit that they were all accepted. The work by Cronbach was placed in the anteroom, while Martinelli's sculpture was mounted on the outside of the east wall of the General Assembly building, overlooking the rose garden, and de Rivera's work is in the office of the secretary-general on the thirty-eighth floor of the secretariat.

Martinelli's work, an abstract design in gold- and bronze-colored anodized aluminum, is a huge piece, 30 by 17 feet. The artist disclaims any "conscious symbolism," preferring to leave any interpretation to the viewer. Yet he himself points out that the "five large amorphous shapes" of the sculpture might be taken to represent the five continents, and the eye of the beholder probably will not fail to detect a fortuitous resemblance between the whole work and the United Nations emblem. The presentation of the Martinelli work was made on October 27, 1961.

The other two American pieces were presented on March 10, 1960. The piece by Cronbach, which hangs on the wall of the anteroom of the Meditation Room, is an abstract design in bronze, representing a sailing ship in motion, and Dag Hammarskjöld, in his acceptance, found in it " . . . a clear association with the sailing of mankind and man through time and through history . . . a strong association with the free horizon of the sea."

The work by de Rivera, a polished bronze bas-relief, is a non-objective design, a pure abstraction in metal, the only sculpture on the walls of the office of the secretary-general.

Art and science are combined in two unusual displays in the main lobby of the General Assembly building—the Foucault Pendulum and a model of the first Soviet "Sputnik."

The Foucault Pendulum, a device offering visual proof of the rotation of the earth, was a gift of the government of the Netherlands. The principle was first demonstrated by the French physicist, Jean Bernard Léon Foucault, in Paris in 1851, when he suspended a heavy sphere from the dome of the Pantheon by a 220-foot wire. A pin was attached to the underside of the large ball, and at each swing the pin swept over a ridge of sand arranged on an inner railing, cutting into the sand. It was observed that the plane of vibration shifted slowly, in a clockwise direction, at about eleven degrees an hour.

For the United Nations installation, a 200-pound gold-plated sphere is suspended from the ceiling at a height of 75 feet. A stainless steel wire holds the sphere in such a way as to allow it to swing freely in any plane. The ball, twelve

The Foucault Pendulum being installed.

inches in diameter, swings over a raised ring, about six feet in diameter, containing an electromagnet in the center. When activated, the electromagnet causes an impulse in the ball sufficient to overcome the resistance of the air and the friction at the suspension point. The sphere thus swings continuously as a pendulum, its plane shifting slowly in a clockwise direction, at the same rate as in Foucault's original experiment. A complete cycle takes about 36 hours and 45 minutes.

This exhibit has proved very popular with sightseers, as has the Sputnik. This model of the first man-made satellite to orbit the earth was presented to the United Nations in 1959, some two years after the epochal launching. The model, which is suspended over the entrance door, had previously been exhibited in several countries under Soviet auspices.

A traditional Japanese pagoda erected just outside the west wall of the conference building houses a "Peace Bell," contributed by the United Nations Associa-

The Foucault Pendulum in place in the main lobby of the General Assembly building.

Visitors to the United Nations examining the model of the Russian sputnik.

tion of Japan. The bell, 39 inches in height and 24 inches in diameter at the base, weighs 256 pounds, and was cast partially from the coins of sixty nations, donated by delegates to the thirteenth general conference of United Nations Associations in Paris in 1951. The bell was completed the following year and was presented to the United Nations on June 8, 1954.

The bell is housed in a structure of Japanese cypress, built after the traditional style of a Shinto shrine. One side of the bell bears the inscription in Japanese: "Long live absolute world peace." The opposite side bears this inscription: "Com-

Renzo Sawada (left), Japanese Observer to the United Nations, and Benjamin Cohen, assistant Secretary General for Public Information, examine the peace bell and pagoda shortly after their installation.

pleted at the Tada factory on United Nations Day, October 24, 1952, by Chyoji Nakagama, member of the United Nations Association of Japan, who, in praying for the realization of the spirit of harmony of the United Nations, obtained co-operation in collecting the coins of many nations. Donated to the United Nations by the United Nations Association of Japan in the name of the Japanese people."

A gift of the government of the United Kingdom is the carved English oak paneling which decorates conference room number eight in the General Assembly building. The decor of the entire room was a contribution of the British govern-

42

Wood paneling, designed by C. T. Pledge, of the United Kingdom, in Committee Room number eight.

Ornamental doors at the north entrance to the General Assembly building.

ment, and the paneling, designed by C. T. Pledge, an architect with the British Ministry of Works, covers one entire wall. The design consists of alternating horizontal bolection molded panels and square fielded panels, the latter depicting eighty-four different designs of English plant and animal life.

Seven doors in the north entrance to the General Assembly building were a contribution of the Canadian government. The doors, executed in nickel-bronze at a cost of $75,000, were designed by M. Cormier and were presented to the United Nations on March 27, 1953, by Lester Pearson, who was then president of the Seventh General Assembly. Each of the seven doors contains four panels in bas-relief, arranged vertically, representing peace, justice, truth, and fraternity.

The United Nations collection of tapestries and rugs has been enriched by several unusual gifts. Outstanding among these is the Mechlin tapestry presented by the Belgian government, which hangs on the north wall of the delegates' lobby. This unique work, the largest tapestry in the world, measures 43 feet 6 inches in length and 28 feet 6 inches in height. Designed by Peter Colfs of Antwerp, whose entry won in a nationwide competition over eighty other designs, the tapestry is woven around the themes of peace, prosperity and equality. In the center of the design, the doves of peace approach the fountain of goodwill, and the symbols of war are vanquished by the symbols of peace and plenty. The borders of the tapestry are enriched with views of the chief cities of member nations.

The dominant color of this masterwork is green, the universal symbol of life and the traditional color of peace. The tapestry was executed by fourteen artist-craftsmen, operating a loom especially built for this project, under the direction of Gaspard de Wit, at the Royal Belgian Art Factory of Mechlin (Malines). The creation of a tapestry of such proportions demands a delicate blend of mechanical and artistic skill, combining the work of the artist, the director, and the weavers. It was necessary to enlarge the small original design to the actual size of the final tapestry, planning the intricate patterns of yarn to reproduce the design and the color. The weavers are themselves consummate artists, and to create this tapestry the fourteen men chosen for the work spent three years in its manufacture.

In contrast to this traditional tapestry is the colorful Kente—a silk African wall hanging—which occupies a position near it. The Kente, a gift of the government of Ghana, measures 19 feet 9 inches by 12 feet 7 inches. It is hand-woven of pure silk in green, yellow, and maroon, with a sea-blue background, and the theme is expressed in the Twi words, "Tikro nnko adjina"—"One head cannot go into council." The design is especially appropriate, since the pattern was originally created in the eighteenth century for the Ashanti Queen Yaa Asantewa, known for her practice of seeking counsel before making decisions. This design has never before been owned or worn by anyone except the kings and queens of the Ashanti.

The Kente was woven by ten weavers in a period of three and a half months,

44

Dag Hammarskjöld, and Fernand Van Langenhove, Belgium's Representative
to the United Nations, admiring the tapestry presented by Belgium.

The Belgian tapestry in place in the south lobby of the General Assembly building.

at the Dento Mills in Nsawam, Ghana, under the direction of Andrews Eugene Asare, and it was formally presented to the United Nations by President Kwame Nkrumah in a personal visit on September 26, 1960.

From the point of view of contemporary art the most interesting attraction in the collection of tapestries is the "Femme sur l'echelle"—"The Woman on the Ladder"—woven by Marie Cuttoli from the Picasso painting, and signed by Picasso. This tapestry, executed in bright tones of green, red, yellow, and blue, measures 78 by 71 inches, and was purchased by the United Nations from a private owner. It hangs at the entrance to the chamber of the Security Council, in the south delegates' lounge.

Two large hand-woven rugs, each 25 by 32 feet, are the gift of the government of Ecuador. Woven in brown and black designs on a natural white background from the wool of Chimborazo sheep, the rugs reproduce traditional motifs of the Jivaro Indians, inhabitants of the tropical jungles east of the Andes. The designer, Hungarian-born Ecuadorean artist Mrs. Olga Anhalzer Fisch, adapted the designs from an actual pattern painted on a bleached tree bark by the primitive tribesmen. Mrs. Fisch not only designed the rugs, but directed their weaving on special looms constructed for the purpose in her own factory. The rugs are installed as floor coverings in the General Assembly building near conference room number four.

Three other rugs designed by Mrs. Fisch on similar motifs are in the first base-

46

President Kwame Nkrumah, of Ghana, presenting a Kente tapestry to Secretary General Hammarskjöld.

ment corridor connecting the General Assembly building and the conference building. These rugs, each 29 by 25 feet, were woven under Mrs. Fisch's supervision by twelve Indian girls in six months, and they were presented to the United Nations as a gift of the National Council of Presbyterian Women of the United States.

A large Persian rug, a gift of the government of Iran, is used as a wall hanging on the eastern wall of the lounge on the second floor of the General Assembly building. It was presented to the United Nations on April 9, 1953, on the same day on which other gifts of rugs were made by the governments of India and Turkey.

The first of two large handwoven Ecuadorian rugs is examined by its designer, Mrs. Olga Anhalzer Fisch, and her husband, Mr. Bela Fisch.

A notable gift of the government of Sweden is the large hand-woven curtain installed in the chamber of the Economic and Social Council. The curtain, designed by Marianne Richter of the Marta Maas-Fjetterstrom Studios in Bastad, Sweden, covers a window area of 25 by 75 feet, and is woven of wool and linen in varying shades of red, orange, purple, beige, and blue. It is the largest curtain of its kind ever made, weighing some 770 pounds.

From the government of Peru the United Nations received as a gift an ancient ceremonial mantle of red material, found in a burial ground in Paracaz. The mantle

The Fisch rugs in the first basement corridor connecting the General Assembly building and the conference area.

A partial view of the lounge on the second floor of the General Assembly building showing the Persian rugs, donated by the government of Iran.

A view of the Economic and Social Council chamber showing the large handwoven curtain donated by the government of Sweden.

This curtain is the largest of its kind ever made in Sweden. It covers an overall area of approximately 200 square yards, and weighs 770 pounds.

is believed to be between 2,000 and 3,000 years old, and was used in the burial of an Inca king. The government of Iceland is represented by a gavel carved out of Icelandic birch by the sculptor Rikhardour Johnson. The design is of four giants, representing the north, south, east, and west, upholding a single burden symbolizing justice. The gavel is used by the General Assembly's First (Political) Committee. This brief summary of the miscellaneous objects of art owned by the United Nations must necessarily touch only a few of the chief items, and many other member states have made modest contributions to the collection.

The United Nations collection is not as strong in paintings as in other areas, and it is to be hoped that the collection will be built up by donation or purchase. Before discussing the paintings now in the permanent collection, a word should be said about the noteworthy project of UNICEF, the agency of the United Nations devoted to the aid of children. Many artists have contributed drawings, watercolors and paintings to this agency, which has reproduced them on greeting cards, of which millions of copies have been sold. Among the artists who have contributed works are Matisse, Miró, Chagall, Raoul Dufy, Henry Moore, Shahn, and many others. This collection is housed in the offices of UNICEF, on the twenty-second floor of the secretariat.

Five of the works in the UNICEF collection are particularly worthy of note. The first of these is a small painting by Henri Matisse, measuring just 5½ by 8½ inches, "The Torch of Hope," in which the artist has symbolized the ideals of the United Nations. The base of the torch is in black, and in the structure of the flame he has painted a yellow crown, "for the fire which purifies and illumines," and a deep blue core "which stands for steadfastness and sincerity."

Raoul Dufy, in a watercolor exhibiting his typical use of delicate pastel shades, has painted the United Nations buildings against a backdrop of New York's skyline. The work measures 19 by 25½ inches.

Joan Miró has contributed a typical drawing, "Children and Birds," in gay tones of red, blue, black, yellow and green. This painting, which measures 21 by 14 inches, has been one of the most popular in the collection.

Perhaps not so well known is Hans Erni, a Swiss artist, whose drawing, "Brothers," also deserves special notice. Done in somber tones of black, mauve and blue, and measuring 15 by 17 inches, the work symbolizes the brotherhood of nations.

A sketch by Rufino Tamayo, painted in delicate pastel shades of blue and pink, entitled "Poésie du Vol," measures 16½ by 23 inches. The work of this Mexican artist is known to many, and this has also proved very popular.

The office of the secretary-general on the thirty-eighth floor also houses a small collection, but since these paintings are on loan from the Metropolitan Museum of Art, they do not properly fall within the scope of this discussion.

The permanent collection now contains paintings from Pakistan, Norway, China, and the United Kingdom. Outstanding among these are the three paint-

Abdur Rahman Chughtai, Pakistani artist, three of whose paintings are at the United Nations.

China, and the United Kingdom. Outstanding among these are the three paintings by the leading contemporary artist of Pakistan, Abdur Rahman Chughtai. These paintings, a gift of the government of Pakistan, hang at the entrance to the delegates' dining room.

Chughtai's paintings are characterized by "a delicate and subtle flat wash technique and a love of linear arabesque." As is true of much of the Islamic and oriental tradition, his work bears a strong relationship to the art of calligraphy. In "Two Women" the artist has used a simple subject to create a quiet composition, with umber, gray, and red rectangles dominant in his colors. The calligraphic influence is seen in the delicate folds of the drapery, the sinuous strands of hair, the outlines of eye and hand, the swinging curve of the scarves. Quite different in subject and execution is "Jehangir and Nur Jehan," in which he has undertaken a royal

53

Dag Hammarskjöld and Professor Ahmed S. Bokhari, Pakistan's Representative to the United Nations, examining one of the Chughtai paintings in the delegates' dining room.

portrait of a Mogul emperor and empress. The poses are regal, as the two look toward a released falcon in flight, and the artist has used smoky colors—orange, brown, and green—and again the calligraphic touch in the folds and swirls of the turbans. In the third of the group of paintings Chughtai has chosen a traditional Islamic theme—"The Sultan and the Saint"—the man of power taking counsel from the man of wisdom. The pure white robes of the old man, his white beard and the staff of old age and wisdom contrast with the worldly dress of the sultan. Yet there is a paradox here, for the sultan is seen contemplating with sadness the blossom he holds, with its one remaining petal, reflecting on the transitory nature of his power and the agelessness of the old man's wisdom.

Sir Patrick Dean, Representative of the United Kingdom, and Secretary General Hammarskjöld inspecting a painting by Stewart Armfield.

Ten Norwegian friends of Secretary General Trygve Lie presented this painting to the United Nations. Seen shortly after the presentation are Mr. Lie, Secretary General Hammarskjöld, Sievert A. Nielsen, Representative of Norway, and Leif Hoegh, a representative of the donors.

Chughtai combines in his work the traditions of the Muslim masters and the contemporary view of art as having beauty in its own right rather than as a mirror of reality. While his work is thoroughly representational, he has nevertheless bestowed upon his subjects modern techniques of abstraction and stylization. His anatomical elongations might be an eastern counterpart of Modigliani or Henry Moore. In his colors also he has combined the eastern love of the bright and radiant with the western romantic tradition. It is a paradox that this completely modern artist is widely credited with the renaissance of Muslim art in Pakistan.

From the United Kingdom came the gift of a painting by Stewart Armfield, which now hangs near the entrance to the office of the secretary-general. Entitled "Vortex," the painting is rich in symbolism, depicting the figures of two men, representing the east and the west, with arms outstretched, irrestibly drawn toward each other in the swirl of a vortex.

The contribution of the Chinese government is in the form of two contemporary paintings by Hsin-Yu, which have been placed in one of the dining rooms on the fourth floor of the conference building. One, in brush and black ink, is a landscape, 24 by 58 inches, divided by matting into twelve sections. The other, a brush watercolor 24 by 48 inches, is a marine scene.

The collection is completed by a portrait of the first secretary-general, Trygve Lie, by the Norwegian artist Harald Dal, which was a gift from a private group of donors.

Measured by the standards of the world's great museums, the United Nations collection is an infant. Yet the world of art and of culture must be heartened by the fact that, from the very beginning, struggling with the giant problems of man's inter-relationships in the atomic age, the United Nations organization and the governments of the member nations have been concerned with beauty as well as the fact of existence. Through the objects of art that have come to the headquarters buildings in New York, delegates and visitors are enabled to see and understand the concepts of beauty that are paramount in lands with widely differing histories, customs, and traditions. Debate in the halls of the United Nations may emphasize the differences between states, but the art on view in those halls emphasizes over and over again, in ways both direct and subtle, the oneness of peoples in the creation and appreciation of beauty. Perhaps that, even more than the delegates' words, may eventually prove to be the cement to bring together the peoples of the world in peace and brotherhood.

Biographical Notes on the Artists

FERNAND LÉGER

Fernand Léger was born on February 4, 1881, at Argentan, Normandy, France. He studied architecture at Caen, and in 1900 went to Paris where he worked for three years before being admitted to the École des Arts Décoratifs and the École des Beaux-Arts. Falling ill in 1906 he spent the winter painting landscapes in Corsica and was strongly influenced by Cézanne. However, his first one man show, held in 1912, indicated a vigorous reaction against impressionism. In the next decade Léger produced a number of ballet sets for such composers as Honegger and Milhaud. He painted his first mural in 1925 for Le Corbusier's exhibition of decorative arts in Paris. There followed exhibitions in many European capitals, and the designing of sets for the film, "The Shape of Things to Come," based on the book by H. G. Wells. In 1940 Léger sailed to the United States to teach at Yale University. He continued to paint while in this country and in 1946 held an exhibition of his American paintings in Paris. In 1949 he produced his first ceramics while he continued to paint and design sets for operas, ballets, and films. It was in 1952 that he designed the murals for the United Nations. In 1955 he won the Grand Prize at the São Paulo Biennale. He died on August 17 of that year in Gif-sur-Yvette. The following year his book *Mes Voyages* was published posthumously with a poem by Aragon, and in 1960 the Fernand Léger Museum opened in Biot, France.

CANDIDO PORTINARI

Candido Portinari was born on a coffee plantation in the town of Brodowski, São Paulo, Brazil, on December 29, 1903. He showed an early interest in art and helped to decorate a church in his native town at the age of nine. In Rio de Janeiro he attended the National School of Fine Arts and later furthered his art education at private academies in Paris. Portinari is best known for his work in Brazil, including murals for several government buildings, among them the Ministry of Education in Rio de Janeiro. His works in the United States include murals for the Hispanic Foundation and the Library of Congress in Washington, D. C. He also contributed a mural for the Brazilian Pavillion at the 1939 World's Fair in New York. His work is presently displayed in museums all over the world.

PER KROHG

Per Krohg was born in Aasgaardstrand, Norway, in 1889. His father was the famous painter, Christian Krohg. For nine years, beginning at the age of twelve, he studied at the Paris academies of Colarossi and Matisse. His first exhibition, in Oslo, in 1907, was followed in succeeding years by shows in Paris, Brussels, Berlin, Copenhagen, and Stockholm. Except for one year spent in a German concentration camp Krohg lectured from 1937 to 1946 at the Academy of Art in Oslo, and since 1946 he has served as professor of art at the same academy. During his confinement at the "Grini" concentration camp on the outskirts of Oslo Krohg conducted a series of clandestine lectures on art for the benefit of other prisoners, before being caught and shipped to a camp in a more remote area of northern Norway. In 1946 this series of lectures was published under the title of *Lectures on Art in Grini Concentration Camp*. Prior to executing his mural for the Security Council chamber Krohg did comparable works in several official and private buildings in Norway. These include the Town Hall in Oslo, the University of Oslo, and the Grand Café, in the same city. He also worked on three large murals for the Oslo "Folks Theater."

JOSÉ VALE ZANETTI

Born in 1913 in Leon, Spain, José Vale Zanetti studied in Italy for a number of years before taking up an appointment as director of the School of Fine Arts at Ciudad Trujillo, Dominican Republic. He has held a number of exhibitions in Spain, the Dominican Republic, Brazil, Puerto Rico, and the United States. He is well known for his murals and has executed more than sixty of them in the last twenty years. As an exile from the Spanish Civil War Zanetti had long hoped to paint a mural that would depict the scourge of war. He devoted ten months to preliminary sketches for his United Nations mural, and five additional months to the actual painting.

BO BESKOW

Bo Beskow was born in Djusholm, Sweden, on February 13, 1906. He studied at the Academy of Art in Stockholm and received further training in Italy, France, and Portugal. Besides being a muralist Beskow is also well known for his frescoes, stained glass windows, and portraits. In the past few years he has executed windows for medieval cathedrals being restored at Skara and Vaxio in Sweden. The artist makes his own glass, using a process he developed after studying the windows at Chartres and Canterbury Cathedrals. Beskow's portraits include three of author John Steinbeck, whom he paints every ten years.

FRITZ GLARNER

Fritz Glarner was born on November 17, 1899, in Zurich, Switzerland, of Swiss and Italian parents. As a child he lived in Paris and various Italian cities. He studied at the Royal Institute of Fine Arts, in Naples, and was active in abstract groups in Paris in the early 1930's. Glarner came to the United States in 1936. Since then his works have been shown at the Museum of Modern Art, in New York, the Biennale in São Paulo, Brazil, and the Museum of Art in Tokyo. A huge mural by Glarner decorates the lobby of the Time and Life building in Manhattan.

PABLO PICASSO

Born in Málaga, Spain, on October 25, 1881, Picasso entered the Academy of Fine Arts in Barcelona at the age of fifteen. Between his fifteenth and twenty-fifth years the artist's prolific output falls into a series of rapidly changing phases. These have been classified, perhaps too strictly, into labeled periods.

After the death of Cézanne in 1906 the younger painters zealously studied Cézanne's work, and for about ten years Picasso was profoundly affected by it. This influence led him toward a complete espousal of cubism, of which he and Georges Braque became the chief exponents.

A neoclassical period occupied the first half of the decade of the 1920's and was followed by years in which the artist completely distorted the human form.

The sculpture and painting of Picasso in recent years have both been characterized by tremendous distortions and complete disregard of normal proportions —in the interest of greater expression and intensity. Today he is generally acknowledged to be the most vitally creative artist of the 20th century.

EVGENIY V. VUCHETICH

Born in 1908, Evgeniy V. Vuchetich is today one of the most prominent Soviet sculptors. For over thirty years this artist has portrayed the heroic image of the Soviet man. His works include monuments to General Gurtiev, in the city of Orel; to General Efremov, in Viazma; to Alexander Matrosov, in Veliki-Luki; and to Belinskiy, in Penza. A monumental work by this artist is displayed at the Permanent Economic Exhibition in Moscow. The sculptor has received the title of People's Artist of the U.S.S.R., and is a corresponding member of the Soviet Academy of Arts.

ANTUN AUGUSTINCIC

Antun Augustincic was born on May 4, 1900, at Klanjec in the Croatian Zagorie. He studied at the Zagreb Academy of Arts and was later granted a scholarship by the French Government to pursue his studies at the School of Applied Arts in Paris. In 1927 he returned to Yugoslavia and became active in a group of artists called "Zemlja" (The Soil). The next year he produced his first large statue, a monument to the Sumadija fighters of World War One. This was followed by a number of other large works including the equestrian statue adorning the Tsar Dusan bridge in Skoplje. In 1936-38 he participated in an international competition in Poland and was awarded first prize for his memorial commemorating the Silesian uprising at Katowice. Augustincic has since won prizes for monuments in Argentina and Albania. The artist has also done a number of portraits, among them that of President Tito.

HENRIK STARCKE

Henrik Starcke was born on April 16, 1899, in Copenhagen. He studied at the Academy of Fine Arts in Copenhagen, and in France and Italy. The artist has executed a number of statues for parks and for public and private buildings in Denmark. Several of his works adorn the Danish Embassy in Washington, D. C.

EZIO MARTINELLI

Ezio Martinelli was born in New Jersey, in 1913, of Italian ancestry. He studied in the United States and Italy, and at present teaches at Sarah Lawrence College, and the Parsons School of Design in New York City. He was awarded a Guggenheim fellowship in 1958. His work is now on view at the Philadelphia Museum of Art and a number of university art galleries.

ROBERT CRONBACH

Robert Cronbach was born in St. Louis in 1908. He studied at the St. Louis School of Fine Arts, the Pennsylvania Academy of Fine Arts, and in Europe. He was awarded the Cresson traveling scholarship in 1929, and the Pennsylvania Academy prize in 1930. Cronbach's works include sculptural decorations for the Social Security Building in Washington, D. C., the Municipal Auditorium in St. Louis, and a housing project in Buffalo. His recent commissions include sculpture for synagogues in St. Louis and Baltimore. A 120-foot bronze sculptured screen by the artist adorns the Dorr-Oliver Building in Stamford, Connecticut. He has had several one man shows and has been exhibited at the Museum of Modern Art in New York, the Whitney Museum, and the museums of Houston, Denver, St. Louis, and Springfield, Massachusetts. He is assistant professor in the Art Department of Adelphi College, Garden City, New York.

JOSÉ DE RIVERA

José de Rivera was born in New Orleans, in 1904. He has executed a number of important commissions and is especially known for his work in stainless steel. His designs include two architectural bas-reliefs for the New York World's Fair of 1939, a large construction for the American Pavilion at the Brussels World's Fair of 1958, and constructions for the Statler-Hilton Hotel in Dallas and Newark Airport. De Rivera's works have been shown at the Art Institute in Chicago, the Whitney Museum, the Museum of Modern Art in New York, Brooklyn Museum, the Metropolitan Museum of Art, and the Pennsylvania Academy of Fine Arts. He won a National Institute of Arts and Letters grant and his work was included in the American National Exhibition in Moscow. Recently he won a Ford Foundation grant for a retrospective exhibition of his work that opened at the Whitney Museum, and will be circulated to other museums around the country by the American Federation of Arts.

HENRI MATISSE

Henri Matisse was born in Cateau Cabbrésis, France on December 31, 1869. As a young man he studied law and was a lawyer's clerk in his native district before going to Paris to take up painting. He worked first at the studio of Bouguereau, and later studied under Gustave Moreau at the École des Beaux Arts. Attracted toward impressionism about 1897, he experimented in the next decade with a variety of colors and forms. In 1907 he opened a school but this was run on conservative lines and lasted only a few months. About 1910 he began to work with the luxurious subtleties of Persian art, diverging from the Cubist movement which

61

had replaced Fauvism. Matisse settled in Nice in 1917 devoting himself to paintings of Mediterranean interiors, still life and "Odalisks." In addition he produced a number of etchings, lithographs, and wood-engravings, including illustrations for several books. He died in Nice on November 3, 1954.

RAOUL DUFY

Raoul Dufy was born in Le Havre, France, on June 3, 1877. He studied at the École des Beaux Arts in Paris and was early won over to Fauve color by Matisse's "Lux, Calme, Volupté." His early work was also influenced by Cézanne, but from about 1912 onward he developed his characteristic manner—light and sketchy in both oil and water-color, a style well suited to gay renderings of such scenes as regattas, race meetings, and theater interiors. Dufy's decorative work included a huge mural for the Electricity Pavilion at the Paris Exposition in 1937. He died on March 23, 1953, a year after winning the International Prize for Painting at the Venice Biennale.

JOAN MIRÓ

Joan Miró was born in Barcelona, Spain, on April 20, 1893. He studied in Barcelona before moving to Paris in 1919, being attracted by the Cubist art of his countryman, Picasso. Miró became associated with the Surrealist developments of the School of Paris and evolved a "sign language" containing hints of a humor similar to that seen in the works of Klée. His paintings are distinguished by brilliant pure colors and juxtaposition of free forms with geometric lines. In 1941 the artist settled in Majorca. He is well-represented at museums around the world, and particularly at the Museum of Modern Art in New York.

HANS ERNI

Swiss artist Hans Erni was born in Lucerne in 1909. At the age of fifteen he began to work in the field of architecture. Four years later he went to Paris to study art, and while there won a number of prizes. In Paris Erni joined the "Abstraction-Creation" group and exhibited with such artists as Arp, Kandinsky, Mondrian, and Moore. Among his better known works are eight murals he executed for an exhibition of city planning in Paris, in 1947, and 12 panels for the UNESCO exhibition in Zurich.

RUFINO TAMAYO

Rufino Tamayo was born in Oaxaca, Mexico, in 1899. At the age of eight he went to Mexico City to live with an aunt. His early interest in art was further stimulated when he began to attend night classes in 1916. The following year he enrolled as a student at the San Carlos Academy of Art. Tamayo made his first trip to New York in 1926 and this was followed by a number of exhibits at various New York galleries. He has executed a number of murals, including ones at the National School of Music in Mexico City, the Hillyar Art Library at Smith College, and the Bank of the Southwest in Houston, Texas. In 1953 he received the Grand Prize in Painting at the Second Biennale at São Paulo, Brazil.

ABDUR RAHMAN CHUGHTAI

The most towering figure among Pakistani artists, Chughtai was born in 1897, of a family known for artists and architects. He is a direct descendant of Ustad Ahmed, the chief architect of the Emperor Shah Jehan. He showed an early interest in art and was briefly associated with Lahore's Mayo School of Art. This was the only formal artistic training he received so that he is almost entirely self-taught. Chughtai worked for several years in Calcutta, painting in the traditional style of the Bengal school, but he soon demonstrated an overwhelming interest in illustrational and "episodic" themes. Early in the 1930's he visited Britain and the European continent for the first time. He became especially interested in etching and worked for many years in this expressive medium.

Catalogue

Color Plates

1. FRESCO
   Bo Beskow.
   9 ft. x 6 ft. 6 in.
   Meditation Room. General Assembly building.
   Anonymous donor. 1957.[1]

2. COMPOSITION FOR CONCAVE WALL
   Bo Beskow.
   Oil. 26 x 14 ft.
   Penthouse, Dag Hammarskjöld Library.
   1961.

3. RELATIONAL PAINTING NUMBER 90
   Fritz Glarner.
   11 x 22 ft.
   First floor lobby, Dag Hammarskjöld Library.
   1952.

4. FEMME SUR L'ECHELLE (WOMAN ON THE LADDER)
   Woven by Marie Cuttoli from a painting by Pablo Picasso; signed by Picasso.
   Tapestry. 78 x 71 in.
   South delegates' lounge, Security Council chamber.
   Purchased. 1958.

[1]Date indicates year of acquisition.

Monochrome

1. MURAL
Designed by Fernand Léger, executed by Bruce Gregory.
30 x 30 ft.
East wall, plenary hall, General Assembly building.
Anonymous gift, through the American Association for the United Nations. 1952.[1]

2. MURAL
Designed by Fernand Léger, executed by Bruce Gregory.
30 x 30 ft.
West wall, plenary hall, General Assembly building.
Anonymous gift, through the American Association for the United Nations. 1952.

3. WAR MURAL
Candido Portinari.
Oil. 34 x 46 ft.
East wall, delegates' lobby, General Assembly building.
Gift of Brazil. 1955.

4. SKETCH FOR WAR MURAL
Candido Portinari.
1952.

5. PEACE MURAL
Candido Portinari.
Oil. 34 x 46 ft.
West wall, delegates' lobby, General Assembly building.
Gift of Brazil. 1956.

6. SKETCH FOR PEACE MURAL
Candido Portinari.
1952.

7. MURAL
Per Krohg.
16 x 26 ft.
East wall, Security Council chamber.
Gift of Norway. 1952.

8. MURAL
José Vela Zanetti.
60 ft. x 10 ft. 6 in.
Third floor, Conference building.
Gift of the John Simon Guggenheim Memorial Foundation. 1953.

[1]Date indicates year of acquisition.

9. MURAL
   Detail of number 8.

10. MURAL
    Detail of number 8.

11. MURAL
    Detail of number 8.

12. MURAL
    Detail of number 8.

13. MOSAIC
    Artist unknown.
    11 x 11 ft.
    Delegates' north lounge, General Assembly building.
    Gift of Tunisia. 1961.

14. MOSAIC
    Artist unknown.
    Area connecting General Assembly building with Conference building.
    Gift of Morocco. 1963.

15. LET US BEAT SWORDS INTO PLOUGHSHARES
    Evgeniy Vuchetich.
    Bronze. 9 ft. x 2 ft. 5 in. x 6 ft. 10 in.
    North rose garden.
    Gift of the Union.of Soviet Socialist Republics. 1959.

16. MIR (PEACE)
    Antun Augustincic.
    Bronze. 16 ft. high. Pedestal 26 ft. high.
    North rose garden.
    Gift of Yugoslavia. 1954.

17. MANKIND AND HOPE
    Finn Juhl.
    Teak wood. 9 ft. 6 in. high.
    Northeast corner, Trusteeship Council chamber.
    Gift of Denmark.

18. PEACE
    Artist unknown.
    Satinwood. 3 ft. high.
    Southwest foyer, General Assembly building.
    Gift of Indonesia. 1954.

19. PROSPERITY
    I Made Runda.
    "Bentawas" wood. 3 ft. high.
    Southwest foyer, General Assembly building.
    Gift of Indonesia. 1954.

20. ZEUS
    Artist unknown.
    Replica. 7 ft. high.
    Main lobby, General Assembly building.
    Gift of Greece. 1953.

21. ABSTRACT SCULPTURE
    Ezio Martinelli.
    Anodized Aluminum. 30 x 17 ft.
    East wall, General Assembly building.
    Gift of the National Council for United States Art. 1961.

22. ABSTRACT SCULPTURE
Robert Cronbach.
Bronze.
Meditation Room anteroom, General Assembly building.
Gift of the National Council for United States Art. 1960.

23. ABSTRACT SCULPTURE
José de Rivera.
Bronze.
Secretary General's office, Secretariat building.
Gift of the National Council for United States Art. 1960.

24. FOUCAULT PENDULUM
Gold-plated sphere, 1 foot in diameter, over raised metal ring, 6 ft. in diameter.
Main lobby, General Assembly building.
Gift of The Netherlands. 1955.

25. SPUTNIK MODEL
About 2 ft. in diameter.
Public lobby, General Assembly building.
Gift of the Union of Soviet Socialist Republics. 1959.

26. PAGODA AND PEACE BELL
Pagoda of Japanese cypress.
Bell 39 in. high, 24 in. in diameter at base.
Gift of the United Nations Association of Japan, in the name of the Japanese people. 1954.

27. DETAIL OF WOOD PANELING
Designed by C. T. Pledge.
English oak.
Committee Room 8, General Assembly building.
Gift of the United Kingdom. 1952.

28. DETAIL OF WOOD PANELING
See number 27.

29. DOOR PANELS
Designed by M. Cormier.
Nickel-bronze.
North entrance, General Assembly building.
Gift of Canada. 1952.

30. DOOR PANELS (PEACE, JUSTICE, TRUTH, FRATERNITY)
See number 29.

31. TAPESTRY REPRESENTING PEACE, PROSPERITY AND EQUALITY (PHOTOGRAPH OF DESIGN)
Design by Peter Colfs.
43 ft. 6 in. x 28 ft. 6 in.
Delegates' entrance lobby, General Assembly building.
Gift of Belgium. 1954.

32. TAPESTRY
Detail of number 31.

33. TAPESTRY
Detail of number 31.

34. GAVEL
   Rikhardour Johnson.
   Icelandic birch.
   General Assembly First (Political)
   Committee.
   Gift of Iceland. 1953.

35. TORCH OF HOPE
   Henri Matisse.
   5½ x 8½ in.
   UNICEF Collection.
   Gift of the artist.

36. UNITED NATIONS HEAD-
   QUARTERS
   Raoul Dufy.
   Watercolor. 19 x 25½ in.
   UNICEF Collection.
   Gift of the artist.

37. CHILDREN AND BIRDS
   Joan Miró
   21 x 14 in.
   UNICEF Collection.
   Gift of the artist.

38. BROTHERS
   Hans Erni.
   15 x 17 in.
   UNICEF Collection.
   Gift of the artist.

39. POÉSIE DU VOL (POETRY ON
   THE WING)
   Rufino Tamayo.
   Pastel. 16½ x 23 in.
   UNICEF Collection.
   Gift of the artist.

40. TWO WOMEN
   Abdur Rahman Chughtai.
   Entrance, delegates' dining room.
   Gift of Pakistan. 1954.

41. JEHANGIR AND NUR JEHAN
   Abdur Rahman Chughtai
   Entrance, delegates' dining room.
   Gift of Pakistan. 1954.

42. THE SULTAN AND THE
   SAINT
   Abdur Rahman Chughtai.
   Entrance, delegates' dining room.
   Gift of Pakistan. 1954.

43. VORTEX
   Stewart Armfield.
   Entrance, Secretary General's office.
   Gift of the United Kingdom. 1961.

44. LANDSCAPE
   Hsin-Yu.
   Brush and black ink. 24 x 58 in.
   Dining room, Conference building.
   Gift of the Republic of China.

45. MARINE SCENE
   Hsin-Yu.
   Watercolor. 24 x 48 in.
   Dining room, Conference building.
   Gift of the Republic of China.

46. TRYGVE LIE
   Harald Dal.
   Secretary General's office.
   Private donors. 1960.

Plates

1. FRESCO

2. COMPOSITION FOR CONCAVE WALL

3. RELATIONAL PAINTING NUMBER 90

4. FEMME SUR L'ECHELLE (WOMAN ON THE LADDER)

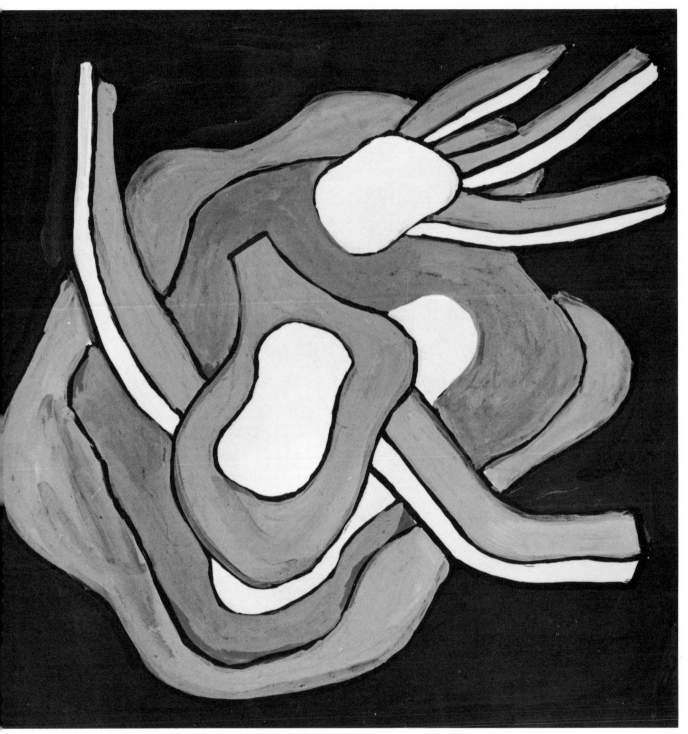

1. MURAL

2. MURAL

3. WAR MURAL

4. SKETCH FOR WAR MURAL

5. PEACE MURAL

6. SKETCH FOR PEACE MURAL

7. MURAL

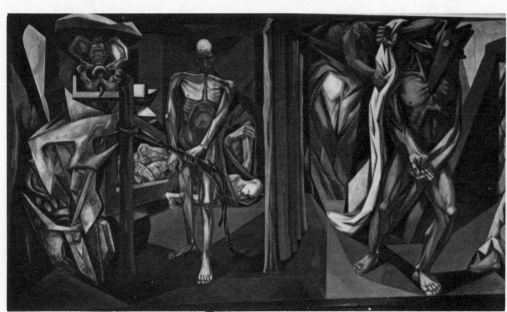

8. MURAL

9. MURAL

10. MURAL

11. MURAL

12. MURAL

13. MOSAIC

14. MOSAIC

15. LET US BEAT SWORDS INTO PLOUGHSHARES

16. MIR (PEACE)

17. MANKIND AND HOPE

18. PEACE

19. PROSPERITY

20. ZEUS

21. ABSTRACT SCULPTURE

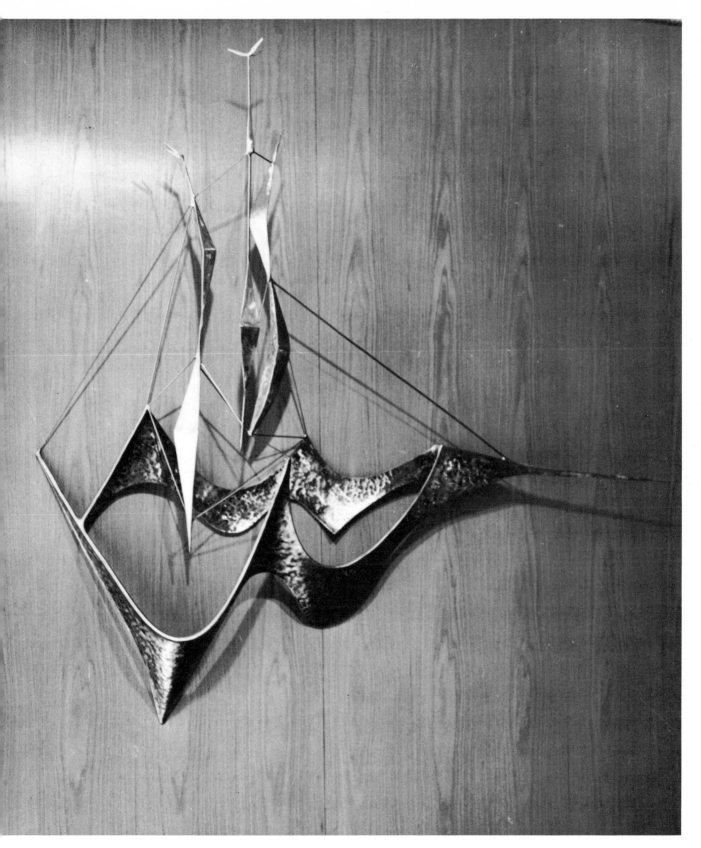

22. ABSTRACT SCULPTURE

23. ABSTRACT SCULPTURE

24. FOUCAULT PENDULUM

25. SPUTNIK MODEL

26. PAGODA AND PEACE BELL

27. DETAIL OF WOOD PANELING

28. DETAIL OF WOOD PANELING

29. DOOR PANELS

30. DOOR PANELS (PEACE, JUSTICE, TRUTH, FRATERNITY)

31. TAPESTRY REPRESENTING PEACE, PROSPERITY AND EQUALITY

32. TAPESTRY

33. TAPESTRY

34. GAVEL

35. TORCH OF HOPE

36. UNITED NATIONS HEADQUARTERS

37. CHILDREN AND BIRDS

38. BROTHERS

39. POÉSIE DU VOL (POETRY ON THE WING)

40. TWO WOMEN

41. JEHANGIR AND NUR JEHAN

42. THE SULTAN AND THE SAINT

43. VORTEX

44. LANDSCAPE

45. MARINE SCENE

46. TRYGVE LIE